Seasons Of Singleness

Nathalie E. Ford

Although the author and publisher have made every effort to ensure that the information in this book was correct at press time, the author and publisher (Maximize Publishing Inc. Nathalie E. Ford) do not assume and hereby disclaim any liability to any party for any loss, damage, or disruption caused by errors or omissions, whether such errors or omissions result from negligence, accident, or any other cause.

The names and identifying characteristics of certain individuals referenced in this publication have been changed. This publication contains the opinions and ideas of its author. Relevant laws vary from state to state. The strategies outlined in this book may not be suitable for every individual, and are not guaranteed or warranted to produce any particular results.

No warranty is made with respect to the accuracy or completeness of the information contained herein, and both the author and publisher specifically disclaim any responsibility for any liability, loss, or risk, personal or otherwise, which is incurred as a consequence, directly or indirectly, of the use and application of any of the contents of this book.

Maximize Publishing Inc.
2018 Monterey Ave
Bronx N.Y. 10457
Attn.: Michael McCain
C/o: Kevin Brown

© 2013 by Maximize Publishing Inc. & Dr. Michael McCain
For Author: Nathalie E. Ford

All rights reserved, including the right to reproduce this book
Or portions thereof in any form whatsoever. Any Reproduction of this book in recording, print or otherwise is punishable by law and copy right standards. For any information or contact with the author you may write the above named address.

**ISBN-13: 978-0615816104
(Maximize Publishing Inc.)**

ISBN-10: 061581610X

Season of Singleness 4

Table Of Contents:

Forward..9

Preface..11

Acknowledgements...............................15

Introduction..17

My Prayer...21

Declaration of Faith..............................23

The Starting Point................................25

Part I
Understanding Seasons Of Life................43

Part II
The Essence Of Time............................59

Part III
Harvest Time.......................................87

Conclusion..99

About The Author................................101

Season of Singleness 6

Seasons Of Singleness

Nathalie E. Ford

Season of Singleness 8

Seasons Of Singleness

Forward

Dr. Michael McCain

I am humbled and honored by God to be a part of bringing this book Seasons of Singleness into the lives of people around the world. Nathalie E. Ford is a powerful and profound orator and communicator. She shares from both a place of wisdom and transparency how to face single living as well as a holy lifestyle.

Seasons of singleness will empower you to approach relationships differently. Through the wisdom found in this book you will be empowered to make Godly choices and liberate yourself from bondages that present themselves in unhealthy relationships as well and heal from past relationships and mistakes.

Mrs. Ford opens up her treasure of wisdom and shares principles and knowledge that will help change the way you think about single living as well as provoke you to understand Gods purpose for seasons. At times we rush through life, there are times we wish we were participating in a different season other than the one that we are experiencing. Through prayer and discipline in the meditations provided for you in this book you will be well on your way to handle your seasons but most of all seasons of singleness.

Be inspired, Be Informed, Be restored!

Seasons Of Singleness

Learning to Embrace the Word of God In Every Season of Life

Nathalie E. Ford

Preface

Life is thought to be a possession that we, as free willed agents, maintain full control of and are at liberty to do what we so desire throughout the course of our lives. Unfortunately reality sets in, and we come to our senses expediently. Often circumstances are simply beyond our control and have not come by way of invitation or a welcome mat, but unexpectedly and unwelcomed. Then there are times when our circumstances are merely us receiving the consequences of our own decisions or the loving chastisement of our father. But if we are going to receive the benefit we must embrace every circumstance as what it is in the sight of God- a spiritual building block. Through these building blocks, we come to recognize our limited ability to resolve the issues and challenges that we face daily and are made aware of our dependence and need for our creator. Without God's proper guidance, life can quickly become an overwhelming ball of emotions, driving you to a circle of confined confusion and stagnation- never fulfilling your true purpose and destiny. But in God there is purpose, fulfillment, and a promising destiny.

God promises that those who cry out to Him in there bewilderment, will find help and the direction they seek.

"For I know the plans I have for you, says the Lord. They are plans for good and not for disaster, to give you a future and a hope. In those days when you pray, I will listen. If you look for me wholeheartedly, you will find me. I will be found by you, says the Lord. I will end your captivity and restore your fortunes. I will gather you out of the nations where I sent you and will bring you home again to your own land."
Jeremiah 29:11-14 (NLT)

Then there is this perspective of what life should be according to the system of the world and the common laws of "success" and "fulfillment" created by humans making imperfect resolutions for a world created by a perfect God. But for those of us who have come to know the power of a redemptive relationship with God through His son Jesus Christ, our eyes have been uncovered from the deception of the god of this world- Satan. We know that our lives do not belong to us. We perceive and recognize them to be a gift that was given to us with purpose, destiny, and a specified perfectly laid path to reach its fullness. A plan created by God that is to bring a future and a hope. A path that will come to fruition in its own time and season only when it has been watered, nurtured, pruned and is ready to be harvested.

John 12:25 tells us *"Anyone who loves his life will lose it. Anyone who hates his life in this world will keep it forever. (NLV)*

In his description Jesus establishes the purpose and principles of life by establishing the need for a "love hate" relationship to the world. Jesus' use of the phrases in John 12:25 illustrates the fact that losing our life is an attitude that values heavenly interest above what is valued on the earth. It requires the willingness to place inconsiderable significance in worldly pleasure, philosophies, successes, values, goals, and sentiments. Jesus reminds us that only those who maintain this type of disposition on life will gain life eternal, and will count nothing in the world so dear that they will not freely give it up for the sake of walking in a divinely purposed life for their Lord.

In this dialogue, we will tap into the understanding of life, the seasons of which we must past, understanding who we are as individuals, and forming a more intimate relationship with God that we may embrace fully the promises which God has set for us in his own time. If we can understand how to embrace the promises of God in the times when we are relinquishing our own will to take on the divine will of God for our lives, we will be empowered to live a ***kingdomfied life- a life where God receives glory, his name is exalted, and his Kingdom is enhanced in all things.***

Season of Singleness 14

Acknowledgements

First and foremost I want to say all glory, honor and praise to God. I thank God for finding favor in me to place his word in my heart, for gifting and anointing me for this task. The journey of experiences that birth the teachings and wisdom found in this book have not all been easy, but I say with all sincerity, I thank GOD for each one. I thank God for favor and grace to endure so that this assignment could be fulfilled. I am forever grateful to God for blessing me and keeping his hand upon me.

Secondly I want to thank my parents, Pastor Willie and Rachel Ford for always being there for me. I thank you most of all for instilling in me the word and principles of God and for your daily strive to live out all you have instilled in me. God truly blessed me by entrusting you to nurture and watch over me. I can never repay you for all you have given and done for me. But I pray that my commitment to serving God and building His kingdom is reward for all you have done.

To my big sister, Coretta Ford-Walker, husband Ja'Ryan Walker, my nieces Jordyn, Tayshon, and Amayri Walker- thank you for sharing your family with me and always supporting, backing, and encouraging me in all my endeavors and assignments. You have helped me stay strong and make it through some of the most difficult times. I love you family.

To all my extended family, friends, supporters, and followers- thank you for your words of encouragement, for recognizing the call of God and anointing on my life. Without your prayers and support, I would not be the woman of God I am today.

Finally special thanks to Dr. Levester Ramsey, Dr. Michael McCain of Maximize Publishing, and Gloria Collins. You all have encouraged and inspired me throughout this project. You have helped push and inspire me through it all. My love and thanks go out to you from the bottom of my heart.

I am forever grateful to you ALL love,

Nathalie

The Introduction

Putting a Face to Singleness

Has there ever been a time in your life when you felt like you were all alone? Maybe you were alone with no one to talk to, no one to lean on, no one who really understood your issues or where you were in life. Was there ever a time when it seemed like no one could comprehend exactly where you were in life, your heart retching pain, understand or grasp your disappointment. Remember when you were in a time of pure complexity and tough situations, but no one came to your rescue, showed up to see about you or just check in on you. What about the times you walked through the church doors, smiled, put on the happy face, but no one discerned the tears dripping from your heart aches. What about the time when you tried to let your husband or wife know how you felt, but they were too busy, preoccupied, or simply just didn't love or even care about you enough to find interest in how you felt at the moment. Maybe you tried to tell mommy or daddy how you felt, or what dilemmas you were struggling with, or about how someone violated you, but they shrugged you off because you were too young to know anything or feel like that. What about the loved one that suddenly slipped from life's battles or was taken away at the hand of someone they or even you trusted. Remember how you felt, like you were dreaming, like life or maybe even God had forsaken you.

That's it- *Singleness* represents those situations or circumstances that left you distinctly different from your surroundings, isolated and desolate; those times when you know that only God could rescue you. Those times that you can recall when you know it had to be a higher power that allowed you to come out without losing your mind, your life, or your family. When you know it was nothing but God keeping you while you passed *through* a storm in life.

At some point in life we will all come to a point when we feel alone or isolated. While our reliance should always be on God in great and small matters, we will encounter a situation or circumstance that will require the hand of God - and God only- to come out. A time when there is nothing humanly possible that can be done to turn things around. I am sure that everyone can recall a time when they felt unrecognized, ignored, irrelevant, overlooked, or just forgotten about. But if you haven't felt that way yet, oh you just wait because you will have your chance. So get ready and be prepared.

***John 14:18* reminds us of this promise, "*I will not leave you as orphans [comfortless, desolate, bereaved, forlorn, helpless]; I will come [back] to you*" (Amplified Bible).**

What consolation we receive, knowing that God promises never to leave us alone by giving us a portion of Him, *the Holy Spirit.* For those who believe in the power, love, and grace given to us through Jesus Christ, we have something to glory in. And what is that you may ask? That is the guiding power, love and grace of our Lord and Savior Jesus Christ. Because of God's undying love for us, He has given us power to overcome every adversity we face. With his precious help, we are and will never be alone.

1 Corinthians 10:13 reminds us that "the temptations in your life are no different from what others experience. And God is faithful. He will not allow the temptation to be more than you can stand. When you are tempted, he will show you a way out so that you can endure".

So not only will He be with us, but He won't allow us to enter into situations He knows we are not capable of withstanding, and then with every situation He will make the way clear to us so we may find our way out.

Understanding where you are is the key to finding the direction you need to move beyond that point and reach your next destination. It's just like a GPS system- in order to give you directions to your desired destination; it has to first determine your current location. Without knowing your starting point, you can get directions, but it may not be the way you need to go to get there. But in life, once you understand your position, your season, your circumstances, and begin to know, declare and receive the promises of God made to you for those times, you will begin to see what path you must take. You will begin to see that God has already heard and attended to your *Seasons of Singleness* cry.

My Prayer

My Prayer for the Readers

As you read this book, it is my sincere prayer that you find consolation in whatever season you may be in……

Read this prayer in Faith and receive its Blessing

Father God I ask that you dispatch a supernatural outpouring of your wisdom and knowledge among the readers that they may rightly receive the words you have spoken. Lord, I pray the spirit of God will tap into every place within each reader that longs for companionship, for validation, for a shoulder to cry on, for a listening ear, for direction, especially for those who are seeking purpose and fulfillment in their lives. Who seek to fulfill your purpose and will for their lives. God fill every empty place and attend to the cries of the lonely and those who feel they are in helpless situations. Let them know that your love alone is enough to sooth any hurt in their lives. Dispatch your love, your power, your spirit among the readers and among your people God. Only you have the power and the resources to rescue them. Equip them with your word and your spirit.

I declare that every stronghold, every curse, every shackle that hinders progression be destroyed. Every yoke of bondage be broken. I curse every seed planted by the enemy, every plot, scheme, and assignment that will try to exalt itself against your word and will, and cut them off at the root. They are canceled in the name of Jesus. In the name of Jesus according to the authority you have given your children to bind and loose I bind every demonic attack and interruption and command Satan to loose every vision, dream, and gift of every reader who touches this book. The blood of Jesus is against you Satan and victory is in the hands of those who believe in the power of God and receive the blessing of these teachings.

Father God let every word you have spoken to me become life. Birth transformed minds, hearts, lives, and healed souls through these pages. Do a new thing in the lives of these holders and readers. Demonstrate your power and show forth a miracle in their lives. Let it not be entertainment God, but let this book be a life changing account that will bring glory and honor to your name and strengthen your kingdom. I give all glory, all honor and all praise to you God, for you have spoken to your people once more. And I thank you in advance for every life that will be changed, transformed, healed, and saved from these pages. Thank you Lord for the accomplishment of your word in the lives of your people. It shall not return void put shall profit for the kingdom of Heaven. IN JESUS' NAME I PRAY.....AMEN

Declaration of Faith

A Declaration for the Lives of the Readers:

Your *Seasons of Singleness* moments are about to come to an end and you shall receive the love, comfort, strength, direction, power, wisdom and knowledge of God. You shall come into a more intimate relationship with God. Purpose and destiny shall be fulfilled in your life and you shall be empowered to live a kingdom lifestyle.

His presence is near you and His Holy Spirit lives in you. Whatever season you are in at this moment is shifting as you read each word and turn each page. Your life will never be the same and you shall walk in the promises of God because you have sought Him wholeheartedly and He has heard and attended to your *Seasons of Singleness* cry.

Believe it! Receive it! Act on it! Walk in it!

The Starting Point
Embracing the Seasons and Times of Life

"And He said unto them, It is not for you to know the times or the seasons, which the Father hath put in His own power."

Acts 1:7

~Understanding God the Creator~

How the Creator Operates

With the creation of mankind, God has demonstrated His power and His life giving ability. When we look back to Genesis 1, God created everything by simply speaking. After creating the heaven and the earth (v.1), He spoke the stars, the moon, the water and dry land, night and day, even the grass to carpet the Earth. He commanded the waters to bring forth moving creatures that hath life, and the fowls of the air. He spoke life into the creatures. He demonstrated that he is *elohim (God in Hebrew)- used in its plural form meaning more than one to show that He along sums up the completeness of all that God is.* David summed up the greatness of the creative work of God in Psalm 19:1 when he proclaimed, *"The heavens declare the glory of God, and the sky above proclaims his handy work"*.

When God was ready to create man, he took a different approach. Let's look at Genesis 1:6 which reads, *"And God said, Let us make man in our own image, after our likeness; and let him have dominion over the fish of the sea, and over the fowl of the air, and over the cattle, and over the earth, and over every creeping thing that creepeth upon the earth"*. The most notable act mentioned in this scripture is the fact that God decided to make man in His own image to represent the likeness to Himself. He chooses to create a creation that would mirror and exemplify His divinity.

<u>The creation of mankind is distinctively different from God's creation of creatures in fact that:</u>

- ***God created mankind to be in His likeness and image so that they would be able to have fellowship with him and be a reflection of Him on the face of the earth.***

- ***That they would have intimate commune with Him.***

- ***In His likeness and image man does not possess the divinity of God, but would reflect His character, His love, His holiness, His moral likeness, and would naturally possess wisdom, a heart of love, and a physical make-up likened of God.***

- ***Finally that mankind would demonstrate his power and authority on Earth by having dominion over everything in the Earth.***

Distinctly, God refers to Himself in a plural form in Genesis 1:6 saying, *"Let **US** make man in our own image"*. But who was God talking to if there was no one of His *"likeness"* on the Earth? He was speaking to Himself. Here God reveals Himself as a trichotomy, having three separate parts. And we know this because man is made in the *"image of God"* and is composed of three parts: Mind, Body and Soul. So that image of man is fashioned after the triune God: *God the Father, God the Son, and God the Holy Spirit* symbolizing the completeness and wholeness of all three that is needed to operate in the fullness of power- the *Holy Trinity. They are three distinctly separate persons (having distinct personalities, character and qualities) yet each carries the same essence of deity and is fully God individually and collectively, yet there is only one GOD. WHEW! Hope you caught that. Simply put, God is so powerful that he had to reveal himself to mankind in three different forms. His glory is so great man couldn't fathom His character if it was only displayed through the essence of one person.* Together, the three persons of the Father, Son, and Holy Ghost set the stage for the divine order of God- which is fashioned in stages of threes.

When God operates in His divinity, He completes His work and shows his power in stages of threes. Let's look at the most profound examples of God's divine work:

God's Redemptive Gift: The Saving, The Redeeming, and The Justifying

1) God's Saving Grace
God loved the people of this world so much that he gave his only Son, so that everyone who has faith in him will have eternal life and never die.
John 3:16 (CEV)

But God commanded his love toward us that while we were yet sinners, Christ died for us.

Romans 5:8 (KJV)

2) Jesus Christ's Redeeming Power:
For it, when we were enemies, we were reconciled to God by the death of his Son, much more being reconciled, we shall be saved by his life.
Romans 5:10 (KJV)

3) Justification's Power Over Death
*Much more then, being now justified by his blood, we shall be saved from wrath through him.
And not only so, but we also joy in God through our Lord Jesus Christ by whom we have received the atonement.*
Romans 5:9,11 (KJV)

Gift of Receiving Salvation: The Confessing, The Believing, and The Receiving

1) Confessing Saving Grace
That if thou shalt confess with they mouth the Lord Jesus, and shalt believe in thine heart that God hath raised him from the dead, thou shalt be saved.
Romans 10:9 (KJV)

2) *Believing in His Redeeming Power*
For with the hearth man believeth unto righteousness, and with the mouth confession is made unto salvation.
Romans 10:10 (KJV)

3) Receiving Justification
For the scripture saith, whosoever believeth on him shall not be ashamed. For whoever calls on the name of the Lord shall be saved.
Romans 10:11, 13 (KJV)

Christ's Future Return- All Things Made New:

1) Mankind Will Be Transformed
But we are citizens of heaven, where the Lord Jesus Christ lives. And we are eagerly waiting for him to return as our Savior. He will take our weak mortal bodies and change them into glorious bodies like his own; using the same power with which he will bring everything under his control.
Philippians 3:20-21

2) New Heaven and New Earth
Then I saw a new heaven and a new earth for the old heaven and the old earth had disappeared. And the sea was also gone. And I saw the holy city the New Jerusalem, coming down from God out of heaven like a bride beautifully dressed for her husband.
Revelation 21:1-2 (KJV)

3) A New Relationship With God
I heard a loud shout from the throne, saying, Look God's home is now among his people. He will live with them, and they will be his people. God himself will be with them. And he also said, It is finished. I am Alpha and the Omega- the Beginning and the End. To all who are thirsty I will give freely from the springs of the water of life.
Revelation 21: 3,6

God's redemptive gift is demonstrated in the act that He didn't give us anything we deserved, have or can ever earn. God looked to the future and resolved in Himself to display His love even before we were created, believed in

Him or even loved Him. He has given us grace; He redeemed us from sin and death through the death of Jesus. Then He conquered death. In conquering death, He took away the need for us to pay for our own sin, rather in lure of our sin; we are offered redemption through faith and confessed relationship with Jesus Christ. Jesus' blood and resurrection was enough to bring life to all of mankind.

Because of the redemptive gift we have a right to direct relationship and fellowship with God. By believing an accepting this gift we are no longer stray children. God looks at who He created us to be and not what we have chosen or turned out to be. Whatever does not line up with His perfect will and plan, God will cleanse and give us a new heart, mind, and forget our past sins and puts us back on the right track. Isn't it good to know that God CHOOSES to forget when we have hurt or disobeyed Him. He doesn't hold our faults against us but is waiting to forgive, re-new, restore, and give us another chance.

The greatest hope for believes is shown in the establishment of Christ future return. We will finally see the savior of the world. The one who gave his life, who suffered and took on all we deserved and canceled our eternal punishment. From redemption and salvation we have the hope of a new world absent of all we know it to be from this day. A new heaven and a new earth will yield us free of sickness, hurt, pain, lack, crime, and give us a place in paradise. Not only will we receive a ticket to paradise as God intended for us to live, but a new glorified body that will be able to stand in the presence of our great God. He will be among his people and live with them. What great pleasure to know that one day the God we have prayed to, depended on, trusted in, and have seen miraculous accounts from will be in our presence. No need for an autograph or a photo to remember by, for we will FOREVER be with God. Oh what joy it will be.

Power Point:

God's divinity work is done in three stages:

- *The Informative Stage- time of preparation or creating*
- *The Performing Stage- time of working or going through*
- *The Manifestation- time of fulfillment or harvest*

This triune God is not God to those who cannot perceive him in his completeness. Each part brings a distinctive need to the Christian life and none can be effective without all three parts working together in unity. One part of the Holy Trinity cannot fully work in our lives without the aid of the others. It is just as the human body would not function without a soul or a mind- it would simply be the dust of the earth from which it was created, useless and of non-effect.

The Giver of Life
"It is the Spirit who gives life; the flesh profits nothing."

John 6:33

Now that we have identified God the creator and understand how He operates in creation, let's take a look at how He brings life to mankind.

Genesis 2:7 says, *"And the Lord God formed man of the dust of the ground and breathed into his nostrils the breath of life and man became a living soul"*.

Now after God created man in his likeness and image, there was one thing left to do…give life.
Here again God does a triune work:

- ***He forms man from the dust of the earth***
- ***He breath into his nostrils the breath of life***
- ***Man Became a living soul***

Here we must identify this pattern to be true to every life giving work God does in our lives. There will be a distinct pattern that God will continue to follow:

A Preparation or Creating - this is point of coming into existence
(Proof: He forms man from the dust of the Earth)

*A Working - this is the fashioning of the creation
(Proof: He breath in his nostrils the breath of life)*

*A Manifestation- this is the harvest or end result of the work of God on and in the creation or time of preparation
(Proof: Man became a living soul)*

We can trust this doctoring based on Malachi 3:6 which says, *"I am the Lord, I change not"* and Hebrews 13:8 which declares *"Jesus Christ the same yesterday, and today, and forever more"*.
God does not change. He will operate in the same manner, fashion, and with the same character He has since the beginning of time and creation. God is not filled with emotional tendencies. He doesn't move because of human emotions, but He moves out of character: healer, creator, deliver, provider, lover, friend, greatness, timeliness, peace maker, comforter, all powerful, all knowing, sovereign, omnipresent, omnipotent, just to name a few. These are characteristics of God and we can expect Him to perform as such. He has possessed these characteristics since the beginning of time, and will possess them until the end of time; that my friend is good news.

What is Life?

Life is defined as:
- *The condition that distinguishes organisms from inorganic objects and dead organisms, being manifested by growth through metabolism, reproduction, and the power of adaptation to environment through changes originating internally.*

- *The period between birth and death; the amount of time something is active and functioning. A present condition state, or mode of existence; the sum of course of human events and activities. The source of strength and animation.*

Let's look at each of these definitions in depth and through scripture:

***LIFE** as the condition that distinguishes organisms from inorganic objects and dead organisms, being manifested by growth through metabolism, reproduction, and the power of adaptation to environment through changes originating internally.*

In this definition, life is characterized by not exhibiting the likeness of :

Dead Organisms- living creatures that are no longer capable of growing, metabolizing, or reproducing. These organisms no longer maintain vitality, are ineffective, and have lost their fire. In spiritual form this could represent a person who practices religion or is bond by religious tradition and has not yet experienced the fullness of having a personal relationship with God. Over time the religious person will lose their ability to maintain their enthusiasm for the things of God. They will become weaker after each life battle rather than gaining spiritual maturity or growth. They will be tossed to and fro with every situation that arises in their live and will never know the true joy of being one with God because they do not have the life giving spirit embedded it them through divine connection with God.

In Revelations 3, God rebukes the church at Sardis for being "dead" in his sight. His rebuke can be found is verses 1 and 2 which read:

"I write this letter to the angle of the church in Sardis, this is the message from the one who have the seven fold Spirit of the God and the seven stars: I know all the things you do, and that you have a reputation for being alive-but you are dead. Wake up! Strengthen what little remains, for even what is left is almost dead. I find that your actions do not meet the requirements of my God". (KJV)

The same type of rebuke can be found made to the Pharisees in Matthew 23; Jesus called them hypocrites, and religious fools who had denied the power of God in their lives. They had a form of Godliness but never came to the full knowledge of Christ. Outwardly the church in Sardis and the Pharisees appeared to be the likeness of having a relationship with God, but inwardly God saw them as being "dead". They only exhibited a relationship with God but in their hearts they were opposite of their works.

We cannot expect to have active, fruitful lives in the kingdom of God outside of giving the spirit of God full control over our lives- allowing him to be Lord. John 15:5 tells us the only way we can produce fruit in our lives is if we remain in God and God be in us. It reminds us that outside of God we are incapable of doing anything.

There has to be a refining in us that will cause us to change, adapt, make use of, and bring forth results from everything that takes place in our lives day to day. That refining process begins from the inside out- our hearts must be opened and our minds must be transformed to the likeness of God. If we want to grow spiritually, we must cut off everything, everyone, every environment, every habit, every tradition, every mindset, and every desire that will hinder our growth- even if it means going back to our roots.

It's just like hair, when it becomes damaged, you must cut off what is damaged, even if it means going down to the root, so that what is undamaged can still grow. If you don't it will stunt the hair growth and eventually cause what is still good to become damaged, never being as healthy as it has the potential to be. Dead leaves will fall off of a tree so live ones can come forth. And we as humans are no different. There comes a point in our lives when we must cut off everything that stunts our spiritual growth to be pruned for our next level in God. It may not happen overnight, it may take some time to fully let go or give up things, possessions, and people you hold dear to your heart, but nothing is worth keeping if it will cause you to be dead spiritually and of no use to the kingdom of God. Cut it off, let it go, put him/her out, lose their number…do whatever you have to do to maintain life.

__LIFE__ as the period between birth and death; the amount of time something is active and functioning. A present condition state, or mode of existence; the sum of course of human events and activities. The source of strength and animation.

This is the definition that best describes our daily day to day events and activities. It is what most people do in this time frame that will cause them to say things like: "man this is the life", "this is living", "life is short", "you only get one life", "live each day like it's your last day". All these phrases point to the fact that "life" is limited in time which no one can determine, and what counts at the end of that time is what we do between the beginning and the end. The truth about life in a time frame is no matter how long or short that time may be, you are not fully active or functioning from beginning to end. There are stages in live which you must past through prior to beginning living- newborn, toddler, youth, pre-teen, teenage, young adult, and then adulthood. These are normally stages, however everyone may not make it through all stages and everyone will start their point of living at their own set time. Some may begin fulfilling their divine destiny in their youth or pre-teen years, while others may be well into adulthood before they begin to see purpose in their lives. The same is true in our spiritual lives.

When we come into fellowship with God and become a part of the body of Christ, we are not fully functioning in spiritual livelihood. There is a period of maturity and accountability that we must reach before God can release us into our full destiny. He has to clean us up and put us on the potter's wheel and sometimes do a total renovation before He can begin to allow us to live in our divine destines. But the love, grace, and mercy of God will allow him the ability to patiently prepare, nurture, and prune us for spiritual things. We come in as babes on milk, (the basis of God's word) and are expected to reach a level of maturity where we can acquire meat (matured understanding and revelation of God, his precepts, and his word).

This was a valuable lesson learned by me in 2011. I had been through a trying year- trying my faith, character, my commitment to God, my motives in God, my obedience to God. I mean everything was tried. I even begin to question if I would ever get beyond the place I found myself confined to. I wondered if I would be able to physically, emotionally, and even spiritually be able to continue in ministry. I questioned me, but God found favor in me. I remembered speaking the words I failed at a lot of things in life, but failure in ministry is NOT an option. Then God reassured me through prophetic impartation that I had not even begun living my life yet. There I was 28 years hearing that I had not even begun living. Wow. Simply put I had not yet matured to my destiny in God. But God's word is sure. His word says whatever work he begins in us he will continue it until it is finally finished when Jesus Christ returns (Philippians 6:1) my life is living proof that the process continues until the return of Jesus Christ. At the end of 2011, I finally found myself at a place of renewal- emotionally, mentally, physically, and spiritually. But then in 2012 I found myself repeating the same vicious cycle. What happened? Life and a weakened spiritual immune system which placed me back on the potter's wheel. But again the faithful favorable God reassured me that 30 was my year of release. So here we I am in 2013, at age 30 and though I haven't fully attained I see the work and promise of God so much clearer. Refining fire doesn't feel good; the gleam that comes forth is well worth the heat.

We won't all get to spiritual levels at the same time. This is an individual walk and relationship with God. Don't be discouraged if someone is on meat and you are still sipping milk, and don't get frustrated if someone is on milk and you think they should be on meat. God has to do the work in us; we must embrace whatever work is necessary to get us to our next level in him-to get us to our fruitful place. Now don't get me wrong, don't get comfortable on milk. Just as milk will only sustain a growing child for so long, so it is with the word of God. Just as a growing child will become malnutrition if feed milk when solid foods are required for its growth, so it is with us spiritually. If we stay on the basics of God's word and never mature our understanding or relationship with God, we will be spiritually malnutrition and will not be capable of reaching our place of destiny. We are children in the sight of God no matter how old we are. That means that we should be continually growing, depending, seeking guidance, and developing a closer relationship every day with our father- or as I like to call him- Big Daddy, because no one is greater!

Life is freely given to anyone who desires it and its benefits. Jesus spoke in John 7:37-38 and declared, *"Let anyone who is thirsty come to me and drink. For the scripture declares rivers of living water will flow from the heart of anyone who believes in me"*. The spirit of God is the only one that can bring forth life and being feed with the word of God is the only substance that will sustain life. Proof is in John 6:63, *The Spirit alone gives eternal life. Human effort accomplishes nothing. And the very words I have spoken to you are sprit and life (NLT).*

This is why God had to breathe into the nostrils of Adam. He had to put His Spirit on the inside of him. God could have spoken to Adam and commanded him to live. He has that kind of power. He would have had life, but he would not have been in the complete likeness of God. But He gave Adam his breath and His Spirit, so he could become a living soul.

Life in the believer comes through experiencing God, his presence, and power in our everyday life. The life that the spirit gives us brings power, fire, and the strength to live fruitful lives- resisting the sinful nature that is embedded in us. As we seek to follow and allow God to be the giver of life, let us be empowered by knowing the truth of what God's word says about the working of the life giving Spirit in our lives:

Galatians 5:16-22-26 (NLT)
So I say, let the Holy Spirit guide your lives, Then you won't be doing what your sinful nature craves. The sinful nature wants to do evil, which is just the opposite of what the spirit wants. And the spirit gives desires that are opposite of what the sinful nature desires. These two forces are constantly fighting each other so you are not free to carry out your good intentions. But when you are directed by the spirit, you are not under obligation to the law of Moses.

When you follow the desires of your sinful nature, the results are very clear: sexual immorality, impurity, lustful pleasures, idolatry, sorcery, hostility, quarreling, jealousy, outburst of anger, selfish ambition, dissension, division, envy, drunkenness, wild parties, and other sins like these. Let me tell you again as I have before, that anyone living that sort of life will not inherit the Kingdom of God.

But the Holy Spirit produces this kind of fruit in our lives: ***love, joy peace, patience, kindness, goodness, faithfulness, gentleness, and self-control****. There is no law against these things.*
Those who belong to Christ Jesus have nailed the passions and desires of their sinful nature to his cross and crucified them there. Since we are living by the Spirit, let us follow the Spirits leading in every part of our lives. Let us not become conceited, or provoke one another, or be jealous of one another.

Where there is life, there is fruit. What kind are you producing?

Reflections:

As mentioned in the scriptures, list anything that may be an indication that you are not fully living in the Spirit of God. Make a list of all habits, mindsets, people, environments, etc. that you believe will stunt or hinder your spiritual growth. Then list what characteristics you can identify that reflect the fruits of the spirit in your life. Pray over this list and allow the Spirit of God to remove and reshape those areas that are contrary to the leading of the Holy Spirit and ask God to sustain and strengthen you in the areas where the Spirits leading is already evident.

Season of Singleness 42

Part I

~Understanding the Seasons of Life~

"Everything on earth has its own time and its own season."

Ecclesiastes 3:1

A season used in noun form is generally thought of as a time of the year: spring, summer, autumn, and winter. The four times of the year characterized by the change in the weather, or denoted and characterized by certain conditions. A "season" is also defined as suitable, proper, fitting, or right time, a period of time when something is best or available. Each season has its own distinct characteristics and each characteristic serves its own purpose for the earth and all of its consumptions.

Aha! Did you see that? Each *season* (period of time) is valuable in its own way and gives what we need to complete the *total package* (the earth and its consumptions). That total package my dear is you and the purpose for which you were created and are here.

In the natural realm of the Earth, each season is for a distinct period of time and is profitable for specific events to transpire in the earth. One season is good for planting, another for watering, pruning and maturing which has been planted, another for reaping the harvest, another for resting. The word "season" can also be used in verb form meaning to mature, ripen, or condition by exposure to suitable conditions or treatment.

When we are talking about life and viewing things from a spiritual perspective, these definitions have direct correlation with what the word of God says about the course of life of the believer. No matter how long each season or period last and what happens in the midst of them, one thing is sure……they are all needed and the characteristics which they provide are necessary for the earth to maintain its purpose. Without one season, the process would not be complete.

Solomon writes Ecclesiastics to give instructions on the purpose and benefit of living a life that is purposed for the edifying to the kingdom of God. Solomon speaks with wisdom and from a personal account. He lived a life which he found to be meaningless and vain in the end. Solomon found himself disillusioned with pleasure and material wealth as a way to happiness. He reminds us that life apart from God is cynical. Solomon had great wealth, power, honor, fame, and even sensual pleasure. He experienced all these in great abundance. But in the end he was unfulfilled and empty. Solomon encourages young people to enjoy their lives, but urges them of the importance of committing oneself to their creator, purposing to keep God's commandments as the only meaningful way of life.

The third chapter of Ecclesiastes describes to us in precise detail what is meant by seasons. Spiritually, seasons are places of condition, of circumstance, of test, of trials, of pruning and purging, of building and tearing down, of blinding and reveling. However, one fact is important and if missed you'll never understand *"spiritual seasons", they* *are all TEMPORARY and NECESSARY*! Once you come to grip that what you have gone through, are going through, and will go through is necessary to get you to your expected end, you will be able to say with faith and assurance - *IT HAD TO HAPPEN*.

Let's take a look at the Seasons of the Earth in the natural scheme and how they affect trees:

Summer
The period of finest development, perfection, blossoming, or beauty previous to any decline.
The key element of summer is its long days and short nights. During the long days and extended lengths of sunlight and access of water, the plants make and store food for rapid growth.

Autumn/Fall
A time of full maturity, especially the late stages of the full maturity or sometimes the early stages of decline (fall).
Key element of autumn is photosynthesis, meaning the putting together of light. During this process plants receive water from the ground through their roots. They also take carbon dioxide in from the air. Then they use the sunlight to turn the water and carbon dioxide into oxygen (needed to breath for life) and glucose (a source of food for energy and building blocks for growing). Chlorophyll aids in the process as an indicator of life by producing a green pigment in the leaves. As autumn begins to approach the days get shorter and shorter and brings urgency to the trees that they better begin preparing for winter.
http://www.sciencemadesimple.com/leaves.html

Winter
During winter photosynthesis cannot occur because there is not enough light or water to generate the process. The trees only hope of survival is to rest and live off of what food they have stored during summer. During winter chlorophyll disappears and the leaves of the trees begin to appear hues of yellow- which represents God's refining fire, and

orange- which indicates transition. Red leaves appear from the glucose (food) stored in the leaves. The brown leaves appear which are made from wastes left in the leaves. During the winter, plants survival is based on how well it has been prepared during the summer and autumn seasons.

In the winter season plants called "annuals" (a plant that completes its life cycle in one growing season) die but because their seeds remain, when spring comes they are quickly sprout up. Then there are perennials which can live more than two years. When winter comes the above ground parts of the plants-it's leaves and stalks- die and fall off, but what is rooted underground will remain alive. It will feed off of what has been stored until Spring comes around.

Spring

To suddenly arise or become released from a constrained position. To come into being by growth or cause a shift. The freshest time of something.

The key element of spring is the emergence of new life. Spring brings forth growth and rejuvenation. During these times the weather conditions are torturous due to the confliction of mixing warm winds from the southern hemisphere and cold winds from the northern hemisphere. When these two conditions mix they produce heavy rain storms, tornados, windstorms, and hailstorms. At the end of the season hurricanes often abrupt with little to no warning. But somehow the earth still remains in its most beautiful state.

http://www.mapsofworld.com/referrals/weather/seasons/spring.html

Now let's look at Seasons from a spiritual and biblical scheme:

Summer

In Proverbs summer is attributed to the small, weak, yet wise ant that provides her meat in summer and gathers her food in the harvest (6:8, 30:25). Proverbs gives illustration of the ant while giving warnings of idleness and slothfulness. As Spiritual creatures we cannot afford to be sluggish or idle especially in the "summer" of life, when the season is profitable for growth and harvest. This is the time in live where the days (victories, abundance, calm of life) are more prevalent than night (trials, hardships, storms of life). It is in these times that we should be building our strength and soaking all we can from spending time in the word of God, seeking his face, in worship, working and building His kingdom. We never know when the season of life is going to change. It's not calculated like the seasons in the earth where we know the season is about to change based on the date and time. I once heard someone say, if you pray during the calm, you can rest during the storm. Let us be wise like the ant and store all we can while the days are long, because there will be a time when the nights will be longer than the days.

In Amos 8, it speaks of a vision of summer fruit. This vision was a vision that revealed Israel was ready or ripe for judgment. The vision of summer fruit was an indication that there time had arrived. Summer is also an indication that a decline is around the corner. The season that follows summer is a season stricken to violence in the earth- hurricanes, floods, tornados are just a few. This is true in our spiritual lives as well. As soon as you get your breakthrough, you make up in your mind to commit to God fully, you make two steps toward God, and here comes calamity; But of course because you have become an enemy of Satan. His purpose is to kill, still, and destroy that which you have obtained in summer so that everything you have stored up in preparation for harvest time will be lost. But thank God that though the kingdom of heaven suffers violent, but the violent take it by force (Matthew 11:12 KJV). We have the power of preservation in God. If you remain in God he will preserve you. He will cause your enemy to stumble and he will rebuke the devourer for your sake.

Autumn/Fall

In this season there is a burst forth of maturity, or completeness. This is when we see the end product of the working of all the other seasons. This is harvest time. A time of reaping what you have stored and sown in the other seasons; when the signs of a mature Christian life begin to show. You begin to produce the fruits of the Spirit, you begin to walk in your callings and gifts, you begin to lead others to Christ, and you begin to be profitable in the building of the Kingdom of God. You will see the answers to long awaited prayers manifest in this season. You will see dreams and visions come to pass.

James 1:2-4 describes this season best for our spiritual lives. It tells us:
My brethren, count it all joy when you fall into various trials, knowing that the testing of your faith produces patience. But let patience have its perfect work, that you may be perfect and complete lacking nothing.

That is reassurance that everything that transpires in life is not for nothing, but it is working in and for us to bring forth a greater good. To equip us for the next round of seasons, so when they are completed we will have everything we need to continue on our journey of life. Though these seasons come repeatedly, they never come with the same elements. But we can be assured that because harvest came in the last round of seasons, that no matter what the elements are in the current round, we are fully equipped to go in and go at it. We are assured that all things are working together for our good (Romans 8:28). We can look back on the previous workings and manifestations of God in past seasons. Our faith will be solid and matured for standing even when it seems like harvest is not coming. Harvest has to come so there can be room for more seeds to be planted. God is a god of continual growth. He will not intentionally allow your growth to be stunted. But what you do and maintain to believe in the mist of your seasons will determine what you see manifest in harvest time.

<u>Winter</u>

Winter is likened to transitioning and refining. During this season the innate changes are visible and are made without hesitation. The change is inevitable. Just as the trees leaves will naturally change color, certain plants will die to be resurrected, and some leaves and branches break away so new ones can spring forth, we will see the winter change in our lives as we grow spiritually. There will come a time when you begin to change- your thoughts, your speaking, your habits, your identity, your heart, your mind, and even your physical appearance. There is just something distinct about a person who has gone through a spiritual transition. They cannot go unnoticed. Just as the trees transition depicts what's happening on the inside- the hidden parts of the tree transcends what is happening of the outside. Romans 12:2 says, "and be ye not conformed to the world, but be ye transformed by the renewing of your mind, that ye may prove what is the acceptable, and perfect will of God". That lets us know that before transition and refining can be seen on the outside, something has to happen on the inside to ignite that change. To grow spiritually it will require a change of heart and a change of mind. We can't see things the way we saw them before we were redeemed back to God. We should take on the mind of Christ being servants for God's kingdom. But if we are going to survive the winter season, we must have something stored up from the previous seasons.

Trees can only survive in winter on what is stored because there is not enough light or water to help the trees survive. Spiritually these are dry seasons- seasons when it seems you can't hear from God, when God has hidden his face from you, when you cannot perceive the hand of God working in your life or your situation. It's a struggle to pray, it's a struggle to read your word or even have an excitement about the things of God. Every believer will go through this season at some point. No, it is not strange. This is a time when God is trying to revive you, build you, and draw you closer to Him. He knows if he always answers right when you call you will never learn to chase after him. You know how it is when you're dating. You don't want to make yourself too available and give the other person inclination that you are there at their disposal. But you want the chase, to fill wanted and needed. So it is with God. He is a jealous God and will have nothing before him. He wants you to want him- both out of need and out of desire. Don't fight the feeling; transition can be a challenging, uncomfortable, and a misunderstood time in your life. But what is evident about transition, is the fact that the reward is always far greater than the process.

Praise Break

Look at Abraham who was required to take his family to a distant unknown land. He became the father of all nations. Then look at Moses who had to stay in the wilderness for 40 years to transition an ungrateful people to a promise land; And Ruth who went into unfamiliar territory in dedication to her mother-in-law after the death of her husband. The lost was not easy nor the transition, but in the end she was rewarded with a great husband, Boaz, and a son. Transition may not be the most comfortable time in your life but, it is one of the most rewarding and beneficial times you will every experience as a child of God.

2 Corinthians 5:17 says, "Therefore if any man be in Christ, he is a new creature, old things are passed away, behold all things are become new".

God desires that we are new in him and he promises a transition and refining for those who are in him. It will not happen overnight and will be a continually growing process for some time. But embrace it, learn from it and know that in Christ you are new: new mind, new heart, new promises, new destiny, and a new eternity. You are new, transformed and refined.

Spring

Finally what you have awaited, spring- the emergence of your new life in Christ. It represents the battle and war now arising between your flesh and your spirit. This is the time after you have made your confession of faith and have committed to living for Christ. When you come to Christ there is a freedom, a liberty that you receive that you cannot find or buy anywhere else. It is instantaneously a gift you receive from God, though many Christians are well into their relationship with God before they begin to fully live in this freedom. Because of our free will nature, many struggle with yielding to the Holy Spirit rather than springing into total submission to God.

I believe the Apostle Paul said it best in Galatians 5:16-17 when he said, *"So I say, let the holy spirit guide your lives. Then you won't be doing what the sinful nature craves. The sinful nature wants to do evil, which is the opposite of what the Spirit wants. And the spirit gives the desires that are the opposite of what the sinful nature desires. These two forces are constantly fighting each other, so you are not free to carry out your good intentions"*.

There is a constant war in Christians that is unavoidable. Our sinful nature will always try to override our spiritual nature but we know that what lives in us is greater than anything that tries to arise in us- the things and desires of this world (1 John 4:4). The adversary of your soul will fight tooth and nail to try to hinder your purpose and destiny from being fulfilled. When he knows he has lost your soul, the only thing he can do is try to hinder you from reaching your divine purpose, tempt you to distrust God and his promises, or keep you bond-never experiencing the joy and peace of God. He will send every obstacle and distraction your way. Your life may seem like a tornado has come and swept away everything that was good and meaningful in your life, or you may feel like the windstorms and rainy days will never end-but somehow through it all you still stand.

That is spring. Though the calamities come, though you are faced with heavy winds and drenching rain, you still maintain your spiritual growth and maturity. You never lose hope or faith, but your mustard seed faith turns it to mountain moving faith. Though your mustard seed faith allows you to stand and grow in all types of weather and conditions in the earth, that mountain moving faith you build in spring will allow you to speak yourself encouraged, overcoming, and conquering your adversary. In the midst of all that happens in spring, the flowers bloom, the grass grows and is its greenest, and new life comes forth. Don't let a little rain, wind or storm keep you from your next place in God. What you develop in spring will take you to another level, another place in God you could not have gone except it been for your endurance of all that came up against you. And because you are still standing stronger than you were before, you know you can walk into the next season with increased faith and ability to trust that God has you right where He wants you and you have been tested, tried, and molded for the season at hand.

Spring forth into your next season. It awaits you and you are equipped.

Conclusion:

No matter what season you may be in now, or what season you are getting ready to go into, the basis of the season rest in being connected to the life giving agent. That life connection is with Jesus Christ and his father. Unless we are connected to him, we will not be able to withstand the times and challenges of each season, nor reap the benefits of passing through each one. Only in God can each season of life be a learning and spiritual building block. Only having the knowledge of his word and the strength and guidance of his Holy Spirit will we be sustained in times when we are perplexed and unaware of our direction or even how to manage day to day. If you want to produce spiritual fruit in your life, you must be connected to the vine.

Get Connected
John 15:1-8

I am the true grapevine, and my father is the gardener, He cuts off every branch of mine that doesn't produce fruit, and he prunes the branches that do bear fruit so they will produce even more. You have already been pruned and purified by the message I have given you. Remain in me, and I will remain in you. For a branch cannot produce fruit if it is severed from the vine, and you cannot be fruitful unless you remain in me. Yea I am the vine, you are the branches. Those who remain in me, and I in them, will produce fruit. For apart from me you can do nothing. Anyone who does not remain in me is thrown away like a useless branch and withers. Such branches are gathered into a pile to be burned. But if you remain in me and my words remain in you, you may ask for anything you want, and it will be granted. When you produce much fruit, you are true disciples. This brings great glory to my father.

We are incapable of doing anything outside of being connected with God. He never intended for us to be alone, isolated in our lives, but he has given provision, promise, and encouragement for everything we face. We cannot know what the future seasons will bring, and it is not for us to understand everything that God has set in his timing and purpose. What we can know with faith and trust and believe is that every season that has been, that is, and that is to come is necessary to grow us up into who God has designed and originated us to be. It is merely preparation to go into greater kingdom work, greater anointing, greater understanding, greater faith, greater love, greater power, and greater blessings. Everything- the good, the bad, the ugly, the unmentioned, the secret struggles, the skeletons in your closet, the self-inflected wounds- they all had to happen so God could do a work in you to produce the fruit of the seeds he planted in you. He had to prune you. He had to strip you. He had to mold you and train you. He had to redeem you. He had to purify and purge you. He had to hide you and protect you for a season before he could reveal and release you. But in the end he will use you- for His glory, for the building of His kingdom. He shall make your name great in the earth so that men will see it, and marvel at the works of your creator and leader. Yes there is an end to your story. You just can't see it now. You may not be able to comprehend how all your mess, your struggles, failures, hurts, loses, and battles will work out for your good, but be assured that God's plans for you are all good and working for your good. Stay connected to the vine and watch God grow and mature you. Even you will be amazed at what God can and will do in you, with you, and through you.

Stay connected to the vine and you will be fruitful in every season of your life.

Reflections On
~Understanding the Season of Life~
"Everything on earth has its own time and its own season."

Ecclesiastes 3:1

Step 1
- Take a few minutes and reflect on situations and seasons that you have overcome and passed through. Write it down.

Step 2
- Find at least one scripture that reflects what God says about each situation or season and write it down.

Step 3
- Now reflect on what you learned, gained, where prepared for or any benefit that came from those situations or seasons.

Step 4
- Now declare to yourself and understand - **IT HAD TO**

HAPPEN. Don't stop until there is peace of mind and until you truly believe that *"it had to happen"*.

Step 5

- Move forward in assurance, a greater ability to trust God, and VICTORY! Find at least three scriptures that will help you remain in faith. Memorize, personalize and expound on them.

Part II

"The Essence of Time"

In order that we understand the duration and purpose of seasons in our lives, let us look at the essence of time in itself. Webster defines time as:

1. *Duration regarded as belonging to the present life as distinct from the life to come or from eternity*
2. *A limited period or interval, as between two successive events*
3. *A continuous, measurable quantity in which events occur in a sequence proceeding from the past through the present to the future*
4. *A predetermined or fixed duration*
5. *An appointed or chosen moment for occasion*
6. *An excepted period of duration such as a day or season*
7. *A suitable period or moment*

We have all heard the phrase, "time is of the essence". This is so true! This phrase not only indicates the limitations that are set by time but also the importance of occurrences at a specified mark or duration. Understanding time in limit and occasion is important when seeking to understand the working of God in our lives and what he has purposed to transpire through it. If we are going to make the most out of what time God has given us we must understand the significance of each event and season which we must pass, know how to handle each season, and be able to apply the word of God in the midst of each season.

Ecclesiastics 3 gave a profound message in regards to the essence of time. As previously mentioned Solomon focused on life and making the most out of it from youth and dedicating it to fulfilling the will of God for one's life. Solomon found it necessary to point out different seasons that one will encounter in life. He makes these points to attest that these events are inevitable. We have no control over them. They are bound to happen and are set in God's perfect timing for each individual. There is no getting around them, no opting out of them, but the requirement of going through and meeting them so that one will fulfill destinies call.

Let it be noted that some of these seasons are not conducive to those who are of the faith, but for each man and woman that is born into the world. The correlating difference is that the believer is the only one who can have a divine understanding about the purpose, necessity, and proper handling of these seasons. It is the gift of the Holy Spirit that believer's carry that will allow the truth of God's word to be revealed to them. Only the Spirit can give revelation of what God is saying in his word.

Let's explore the seasons and life events which Solomon spoke of and see what God has to say about them.

Verse 2:
"A time to be born, And a time to die; A time to plant, And a time to pluck what is planted."
Consistency of Change

Solomon's account here is the principle that there is a beginning and ending to everything in live and in the earth. He reminds us that nothing is permanent but is fixated for a limited duration. Every person that comes into your life will eventually leave your life, rather it be through appointed time or through the breaking of a relationship, distance or personal growth. Every job will come to an end rather through promotion, demotion, termination, change of heart, or failing of a business plan. Every tree and plant will eventually be cut down rather it be because of its inability to produce life, the wrath of the elements, or its distant need or incompatibility with its new found surroundings.

This same principle is needed to understand that there will be a beginning and ending to every spiritual season in our life. We will be in a consistency of change, growth and maturity as we grow in Christ. As we become more like Him, there will be a constant revolving of change taking place. This is necessary so we do not get comfortable and stagnant at times when we feel we have peeked spiritually. As we grow and mature God wants to use and elevate you to greater heights so you may be more effective in spreading his good news and leading others to Christ. He doesn't want you with the same mindset, abilities, and resources you came to him with. No! He wants to multiply and perfect all that you have and all that is within you.

Just as moving too quickly in spiritual things can be detrimental to the fulfilling of one's purpose and destiny, so can being out of sync with the move of the spirit and staying in one season to long. We have to be willing to welcome change and say good-bye to the familiar with no regrets and no looking back.

Verse 3:
"A time to kill, and a time to heal. A time to break down, and a time to build up."
Understanding Forgiveness

Here Solomon depicts a great picture of the constant strategy for spiritual growth. As we mature and seek more and more after God and to become more like Christ, there will be a revealing of things which hinder us. There will be insight of familiar things, people, habits, mindsets, traditions, lifestyles that we will be able to recognize as plots, distortions, lies, and tricks from the pit of hell to kill, steal, and destroy our purpose and our soul. Because we know these things originate from the enemy of our souls, I must take on a mindset of war, captivity, and restoration. This is the strategy Solomon gives to believers in this season of live.

When the blinders are taken off and the spirit of God reveals truth we must be ready to "kill"- to deprive some things of producing in our lives. To destroy works, to do away with, to cause every hindrance in our lives to DIE. This means searching and digging to the root cause of behaviors, mindsets, failures, fears, searching out the true condition of our hearts. You may have to go back as far as your childhood to the playground, but you must go back to find the root. If you can kill the root then everything attached to it will die. Mark 3:27 says *"No man can enter into the strong man's house, and spoil his goods, except he will first bind the strong man; and then he will spoil his house."*.

Finding the solution to any problem in life first beings with determining the cause of the problem; Without knowing the cause, you can't recognize the affect, without the affect you cannot determine an accurate plan of resolution. In order for the healing to take place the solution must be active and completed. Once the problem is solved them the healing can begin. Spiritually speaking once we determine what needs to be killed, find the root, and then we can take action according to the principles in the word of God. We can initiate the power and instruction of the Holy Spirit to tear down those things which have kept us bond for so long and has kept us bond, unfruitful and living outside of the divine will of God for our lives.

When we allow God to root out and heal, the by product is restoration. When something is being restored, it is not made from new or from scratch, but you take what you have, tear away what is old, worn, not useful, or not needed to begin the restoration process. You don't get rid of what you have you simply do whatever is necessary to bring back the original state. When God restores, He is merely bringing back life to His original design for our lives. He is reestablishing our relationship with Him and ability to follow His will. He is bringing us back to our original state of righteousness. He is bringing back health to our souls and soundness of mind. He is restoring so that you can continue in His original purpose and to carry out His original plan for your life.

In this season you may see some meaningful places, people and things disappear in your life simply because they are no longer relevant or hold divine purpose in your life. Be willing to let lose any and everything no matter the cost. You'll be astounded at what comes out of a vessel restored to its original state. Always remember as time passes gold restored and refined to its original state becomes more valuable than gold found new. It's simple a refining and God wants you to be as pure gold…your more valuable to the kingdom that way.

What is God asking you to let go so that He can revive and restore you?

Verse 4:
"A time to weep, and a time to laugh; A time to mourn,

and a time to dance."
Joy and Cleansing

As life progresses we will past through periods of hurt, of disappointment, of grief, sorrow, of emotions that are overwhelming and can easily lead to depression, anger, bitterness, or un-forgiveness that will taint our hearts and cause our spirit to be grieved. Tears in these times, when we cannot verbally make an outward expression, can provide a release of emotions, grieves, and feelings that are otherwise inexpressible.

David vigorously cried out to God in distresses. In Psalm 42 David declared that his tears had become his food day and night while they said to him where your God (verse 3) is. David proves here that the emotions he felt that required him to cry out were not from intense spiritual awakening but taunting of demonic vapors. He had to release those vapors. Once David released those vapors He remembered the joy he once had he remembered the praise he once rendered (Verse 4). Once he was cleansed he came to himself and begins to cast down those emotions that were sent to taint and destroy his soul and begin to speak life into him-self. David said, "Why are you cast down, O my soul? And why are you disquieted within me? Hope in God, for I shall yet praise Him for the help of His countenance (verse 5).

Tears are a cleansing for the soul. It rids the soul of vapors that long to grip us into spiritual traps that keep us bond to emotional ties. Tears are like an intercessor between our souls and our spirits; Tears interpret our feelings and emotions and displays them though weeping. The tears act as a cleansing of the soul to rid the spirit free and interrupt any vapors the enemy tries to send through the air to contaminate us that will cause our bodies to be lead to sin and separation from God. Mourning is expressed often through weeping. It displays a sorrow, a feeling of regret often associated with loosing, of disappearance, or separation from something. Without tears the soul is never cleansed and we risk our spirits being contaminated with evil emotions.

There will be a time in everyone's life when weeping is simply necessary. It is not uncommon nor is it wrong. Some may weep more than others some may seldom weep but if you want your soul to be cleansed you must weep. You must allow the cleansing to take place so you may live in the freedom and liberty of the spirit. God has given a promise to those who sow in tears. Weeping is sowing; you're giving of something to receive something. Your giving your sorrows, your pain, your hurt, your fears over to God and giving Him free room and course to restore to you joy, peace, confidence, and every good thing that He has for you. Psalms 126:5-6 promises *"Those who sow in tears shall reap in joy. He who continually goes forth weeping, Bearing seed for sowing, shall doubtless come again with rejoicing, bringing his sheaves with him"*.

Once the weeping has ended and the cleansing has begun. Then we can experience joy. Laughter is a sign of joy to the believer. Laughing as Solomon depicts is simply the presence of joy. To have joy is to have the spirit of God active in your life, in your situation, in your circumstances. This laughing is a sign that life has been brought back to our spirit man and is a sign of victory over the vapors of satanic attack. It is a victory shout in the spirit. It is an expression of freedom. Only the spirit alive in you can bring about this kind of expression. That laughter may not be expressed in an out loud outburst but can be evident based on the way we operate in the midst of circumstances and trials. Every believer should long and work toward living with this joy day to day. The more we learn to recognize those vapors the less we will be lead to have a need to weep and mourn and the laughter, the joy will be every present in our daily lives.

Go ahead weep and mourn if you must, but know that your cleansing will spring forth joy and laughter to your spirit and to your life.

~~Weeping may endure for a night but JOY IS COMING in the morning. ~~

Verse 5:
"*A time to cast away stones and a time to gather stones, a time to embrace, and a time to refrain from embracing.*"
Fasting and Prayer

Solomon took a totally different route on me here. It has taken some time for me to understand clearly what God is saying through Solomon here....but here we go. I don't know if this will seem strange to you, but it did to me at first. But thank God for the revealing power of the Holy Spirit. Here what Solomon is referring to is the principle of fasting and prayer, but as a means of warfare. Bear with me as I relate this to you and I pray the Holy Spirit will break it down in a manner that will be enlightening to everyone.

First let us focus on stones. Focusing on the *nonmetallic mineral* component of stones of which *rock* is made we find that the byproduct of these minerals, which need refining before use, are generally used for building materials; These hard, solid, nonmetallic mineral matters are matters that do not yield a new product when melted or when under heat. They do not shine or have a luster of their own. When they are hit they will break into pieces. These stones are the elements that are broken away from a rock. They are portions or fragments of a larger rock. Without the rock there would be no stone.

This definition describes similar attributes of a Christian life, of a vessel ready for use of God. The refining that God does in our lives is for building. Before we can ever be used of God He has to do a refining within us which begins from the day we acknowledge Jesus Christ as our Lord and Savior. When you come to God He has to gut you. He has to clean out everything that would cause you lose your savior. It's just like going fishing. No matter how many fish you hook to your line, you'll never be ready to fry them until you clean and gut them. When God guts us He only leaves that which is profitable and suitable to live a life according to His word; Qualities that will cause you to remain strong in the heat of the refining fires. Most importantly we don't shine on our own. We are the light of the world but only because of the Spirit of God that lives within us. We have to have his Spirit in us renewed so that we may maintain our luster.

For believers, the way we make it through the refining, the gutting, and the polishing is to adopt a lifestyle of continual fasting and prayer. Fasting requires a sacrifice. We know from the history of the Bible that there was a sacrifice offered to God, there was a blessing. That sacrifice allows us to cast aside anything that would block or distract us from being in the presence of God. In fasting you place yourself in a position to fully rely on the Spirit of God that is within you to become active. The Spirit is stirred in you to help you maintain the sacrificial restrictions that would give Him room to work. Fasting is often done to bring outward reward that is sparked by inner change.

Prayer is simply your communication with God; whether it is you pouring out your heart, offering praise, our pleading your case. Prayer allows you to freely express yourself to God; it's not that He doesn't know everything already, but it lets Him know that you trust His insight, that you feel connected to Him, and that you realize your own inability to deal with your request on your own. In prayer you can seek the face of God to know Him better and to become more like the attributes of His son. Prayer is a petition that brings great reward and great increase for our spiritual lives.

Coupled together fasting and prayer are one of the most powerful weapons that we have in our daily walk because you relinquish your own strength, thoughts, and plans and open your Spirit man to receive an increase in power. Through fasting and prayer you build spiritual muscles. Those muscles help to exercise your faith and believe. Without your muscles you would not be able to hold up against the forces of evil that come to destroy you and your future destiny.

Solomon reminds us that in fasting and prayer there may be times of need for corporate fasting and prayer- gathering stones and embracing, and then there is a time for individual fasting and prayer. Corporate fasting and prayer is generally to unite a particular segment of believers to a specific spiritual cause of which God is sought. The benefit is that the body of Christ is edified. Individual fasting and prayer is generally done to help the believer to build their relationship with God and to seek after God for a specific need or request. During individual fasting and prayer, the individual is strengthened, but may be strengthened in such a way that others in the body of Christ receive just as much benefit from that one person's sacrifice.

Fasting and prayer are the stones that help build the solid foundation of spirit and word in the believers life It produces character that is liken to a good builder. The foundation that believers need is made of spirit and word. Matthew 4:4 reminds us that man should not live by bread alone, but by every word that God spoke. It is solid, it is proved, and it is sure. There comes a time the believer's life when the simple fact that God said "it" has to be enough for belief to take place. The Spirit of God working to bring the word alive in your life will allow you to be a fruitful productive believer who sees the word manifest in your life. You will see the promises of God's word evident in your life. The more you fast and pray the more you will long for the presence of God, the more you will desire to seek His face realizing that there so much that can be found in the presence of God. You will love Him more, you will walk more like Him, you will love more like Him, forgive more like Him. Simply put, you want more of Him; get in His presence through denying your flesh and feeding your spirit through fasting and prayer. You will love the rock that is formed out of the refining, gutting and polishing of the stone you go to Him as.

Verse 6:
"A time to gain, and a time to lose; A time to keep and a time to throw away."
Binding and Loosing

Gain, lose, keep, and throw away. These are words that are not easily received in today's culture. Being the self-sufficient and self-seeking people that we have become the thought of losing and throwing away may give some a bitter taste and even lead them to turn away. But I can assure you that these principles and requirements of kingdom living are just as profound as any other. Before I go any further with this text, I want to remind you that in GOD there is no lose. For whatever God requires or removes He does so only that something greater, better, and more efficient for your life can come forth. God will never require us to lose anything that He himself is not willing to replace.

In this scripture I am immediately drawn to Matthew 16:19 which says *"And I also give you the keys of the kingdom of heaven, and whatever you bind on earth will be bound in heaven and whatever you loose on earth will be loosed in heaven."* NKJV While some may see gaining, losing, keeping and throwing away as a principle they would like to avoid, it is actually a principle of authority and access. Wow did you see that, God is actually releasing to you access and then the authority you need to over through, call to existence, and bring Heaven to Earth. Who wouldn't want that kind of authority and access in their daily life. Just imagine feeling lonely then casting down (binding, losing, throwing away) loneliness and calling forth (loosing, gaining, keeping) peace and worthiness in your life and heart. Well you do. You have the authority to command your atmosphere, your environment, your thoughts, your actions, and your life. You have that authority, you have that right, and you have access. It is yours for the taking.

Understand that authority gives you qualities and tools that you will need for everyday life and every spiritual battle you will face along lives journey. Authority gives you power to determine or settle issues or disputes. It gives you the right to control and command all that concerns you. It gives you a legal right to command, settle, and determine according to the principles of God. With God given authority there is nothing that you cannot overcome. We often walk in defeat because we do not understand the authority that God has given to His children. From the beginning of time, back to Genesis, when God created all things, He gave authority to Adam and Eve over every living thing. That same right was given back to us during our redemption through the birth, crucifixion, death, burial, and resurrection of Jesus Christ. When He rose declaring all power in His hands we received that authority to have and be all that God originally planned and designed for our lives.

You may say well if this is true then why are there so many defeated Christians. The answer, because we have denied ourselves access to the right of authority. Yes. We have denied ourselves access. The promises of God are yea and amen, the reason we don't get the yea and amen is simply because we don't fulfill the requirements that yield the yea and Amen. God is a God of order, he designed it that way and He operates that way. Even His love was displayed in a specified order. He had to first love us, then he had to give to redeem us, then after he redeemed us, he gave us access back to the kingdom.

If we want to know how to gain that access we must go back to the text of scripture in Matthew 16. Going back to verse 13, we see Jesus posing a question to his disciples. He inquired of them there confession. There comes a time when we have to express our confession. When you arise in the morning you have to make a choice, you have to express your confession of who God is in your life in your current situation. In the midst of every obstacle and trial, every temptation you must submit your confession to it. You must understand that the power of authority and confession comes from having a clear understanding of who God is, His nature, His character, and His love. Yes there are things the human mind will never be able to comprehend, but we must rely on the revelation already given to make our determinations. We get these revelations directly from the scripture, from the word of God. The word is alive and so is our God.

Jesus reminds us that it is just as important that our confession be correct. When Peter confessed Jesus to be the Christ, the son of the living God (verse 16), Jesus replied that a blessing was extended to Peter (verse 17). That blessing was the fact that Peter expressed an undeniable faith in God. Jesus told Peter that his confession was not based on what he saw but what He believed (verse 18). Peter's faith in this passage exemplifies the importance of faith to maintain a solid Christian foundation. It is that foundation of faith that leads us to a right confession, which in turn leads us to receive access that is needed to exercise the authority God has given to His children (verse 18-19). For believes today this is where the Holy Spirit comes in to work in our lives. It is the evidence that the spirit of God is at work in our lives revealing and communicating with us. We cannot have a solid foundation of word or confession without the work of the Holy Spirit for it is the living being the reveals, establishes, and gives life to God's word in our hearts and lives.

You see we have the authority to overthrow, to rid, to hinder, to cast down, to deploy and destroy every work, thought, action, diagnosis, stronghold, and generational curse that has lingered for so long in our lives or families. But we have to establish a faith built confession that will put us in position to exercise the authority that is ours. We have the power to command the fruits of the spirit evident in our lives, to engage in successful spiritual warfare in this age, but we first have to get and maintain that access that is necessary through confession, faith, and the working of the Holy Spirit to empower, lead, and direct us in all things.

Do you have access to the authority available to you?

~~~~~~~

Take a few minutes here to search out the scriptures to see who God is, His nature, His character, and His love then journal what you find so that your confession may be strong and effective.

~~~~~~~

Verse 7:
"A time to tear, And a time to sew: A time to keep silence and a time to speak."
Who's report will you believe?

The closer we get to the end of this passage of scriptures, it seems the requirements are becoming greater. Now here we are tearing and sewing, silencing and speaking. But these are also vital practices that will help when going through the seasons of life. It has it's great rewards and if embraced, will yield a mighty warrior in you.

Throughout life there will be many times when we are presented with facts, with opportunities, with the wisdom and sense of man. There will be times when we are tempted to give in, to speak against something or someone, and verbally release promises made to us by God. Nothing is wrong with any of these situations, but the key to making the most and getting the profit out of them all is timing, the knowing when and when not to, and understanding the releasing and the embracing.

From birth there will be people labeling you, judging you, pronouncing there theories over you, telling you what you can and cannot do or be, what you should or should not do or be. They may be some of the most special people in your life, or even the closet. But what you must always grab hold to is the truth of who God says you are, what He says you should do, what he says you shouldn't do, what he says you can and cannot have. Take those principles and run with them. God has given us many promises and accounts of His plan for his children, his heirs. He may not have laid out the specifics to each individual life in the bible, but he makes His ultimate goal, statues, and principles pretty clear in His word. And the end result is good and abundant life.

God has promised his children power, authority, spiritual and physical prosperity, health. He promised to bless them for thousands of generations. Yes these are just the beginning of the promises of God for his children. He promised that they would be rejected as He was rejected, scorned, rebuked, suffer trials and tribulations, he promised chastisement, and correction when they error in their ways. Yes even these promises are good. Every promise of God is good; we just have to put everything in its proper perspective. This brings me to the very important question of this segment…..*who's report will you believe*?

With that question, I am pressed to go to what I consider to be the greatest account in the bible regarding the promises of God and believing only what he says. Let's go to the Promised Land. In Numbers 13:2 we see God making a promise to Moses that he would give the children of Israel the land of Canaan. God instructed Moses to send spies into the land. When Moses sent out the spies to observe the land, he instructed them on the specifics to look for in the land and to bring back a full report (verses 17-20). When the spies retuned they reported that the land was just as it was spoken, it flowed with milk and honey and they brought back great fruit taken from the land. Even though they saw the promise of God as true, they still believed that they were incapable of receiving the promise. 10 of the 12 spies reported that they appeared as grasshoppers in their own sight, they would never be able to take the people of the land. But 2 spies, Caleb and Joshua believed that they would possess the land because the Lord promised them.

After the report was given the people decided that they were not able to conquer the land because they believed the report of the majority of the spies rather than believing the report of the Lord. They walked in unbelief. Even though God had proven himself faithful in the years they spent in the wilderness and in their deliverance from Egypt, it still wasn't enough the break the evil report of the vast majority of the spies. It was their unbelief that caused them to miss their promised land. In Chapter 14 God concluded that no one who disbelieved would enter into the Promised Land. Only Joshua, Caleb, and the descendants of the other 10 spies would enter into the Promised Land.
(For deeper insight read Numbers 13-14)

Here this brings us back to the question *who's report will you believe?* Unbelief is a thief that comes to rob you of all that God has for you. It wants you to believe that you can't have or be what God says. It will have you discount the power and authority of God to perform what he says. It will cause you to distrust the fact that all God speaks is truth. It will even have you question your relationship and ability to hear and obey God. Unbelief is a product of the enemy himself who is the father of lies.

God reminds above all that unbelief is a breach in the covenant agreement He has made with his children. He warned them that because of their infidelity, their sons would be shepherds in the wilderness forty years. The fact that the word infidelity is used, reminds us that God's promises to his children are based on a covenant agreement. To disbelieve what God has promised is to break the covenant you have to stand in faith with him. We enter into this covenant through believe in faith and remove ourselves from receiving the blessings of the covenant by unbelief and wavering in faith.

This is where the tearing and sewing, keeping silent and the speaking come into play. It is so important that as believers we stand on what is truth and not just what majority of Christians or religious fanatics say. It's important that we understand that even that facts do not supersede the promises and spoken word of God. If it isn't the truth of God's word they renounce it. Renouncing is the tearing. You disown the facts and replace them with the truth of God's promises. Renounce what even may make sense regarding your situation and replace it with what God speaks regarding the matter. Understand the facts of the doctor's report, understand that facts of your financial situation, understand the normal outcome for those who are brought up in a nontraditional household or from broken homes and misguided parental figures. But know what God's promises are for those who trust and are in covenant relationship with him. We as believers have to maintain a daily lifestyle of walking by faith and not by sight.

We are also to protect our ear gates from what we hear. Often what we hear will determine what we will begin to speak out of our mouths. Just like the children of Israel, they spoke and believed what they hear the most. The majority said impossible and only two said possible. So they chose the facts over the promise. There is a time to speak and a time to keep silent. If you know the promise of God then you need keep silent and not come into agreement with anything that is contrary to what God has spoken and combat it with the truth. 2 Corinthians 10:4-5 tells us "For the weapons of our warfare are not carnal but mighty in God for pulling down strongholds, casting down arguments and every high thing that exalts itself against the knowledge of God, bringing every thought into captivity to the obedience of Christ (NKJV)". There you have it, we must take control of our thoughts. If we are going to win this battle of speaking and agreeing with only what is truth according to the word of God, we must do so by first taking captive our thoughts. The arena of the mind is where every battle is won or lost.

Walking in faith may not always be the easy position to take. Let's be honest, in hind's sight it sometimes may seem easier to give in or stop believing because there seems to be an easier or more logical way to reach or promise land. But we know what happen to the children of Israel when they decided to take a short cut, it extended a few days journey to a 40 year journey of constant faith testing and still most did not make it to the promised end. Bottom line, though it may not always be the more logical way out in our sight, we can trust that God's way is always the best way. And when you truly desire to live for your father, in the end you will do what He desires and designed no matter how you try to get around it. In the end you will land exactly where He intended for you to be.

Focus Points:
What is God's report concerning your life?

- *Take a few minutes and search the scriptures to see what God says about the promises He has made to those who are in relationship with Him.*

- *What do they promise?*

- *Now spend time in prayer seeking God for specific promises for your life and destiny. What does God say about you as an individual? What does He have planned for you?*

- *What reservations do you have concerning God's promises concerning you?*

- *How can you overcome those reservations?*

Focus scriptures to Keep You Believing

Psalm 27:13-14 (NKJV)
"I would have lost heart, unless I had believed that I would see the goodness of the Lord in the land of the living. Wait on the Lord be of good courage, And He shall strengthen

your hearts. Wait I say on the Lord!"

Lamentations 3:21-26 (NKJV)
"This I recall to my mind, therefore I have hope. Through the Lord's mercies we are not consumed. Because His compassions fail not. They are new every morning. Great is Your faithfulness. "The Lord is my portion," says my soul, "Therefore I hope in Him!" The Lord is good to those who wait for Him, To the soul who seeks Him. It is good that one should hope and wait quietly for the salvation of the Lord.

Psalm 37:3-5 (NKJV)
"Trust in the Lord, and do good: Dwell in the land, and feed on His faithfulness. Delight yourself also in the Lord, And he shall give you the desires of your heart. Commit your way to the Lord, Trust in Him, And he shall bring it to pass."

Verse8:
"A time to love, And a time to hate; A time of war And a time peace."
The Violent take it by force

As we conclude the seasons of life, we enter into end result to the seasons…Living a kingdom lifestyle of spiritual warfare. Every day that we awake, we have to make a choice of who we will serve. God or Satan; if we will chose to follow our own will and desires or the perfectly laid plain God has specifically designed for us.

Whatever choice we make we must remember that there is an adversary who has one purpose- he wants to kill, still, destroy you, your future, and your ability to tear down his kingdom. While he is not all powerful, we must not discount Satan's ability to maneuver and manipulate you into getting off track. He will try all he can to take your focus off of kingdom building and kingdom tearing. Just as sure as he doesn't want you to tear down his kingdom, even more he does not want you building God's kingdom.

If we are going to combat the trickery and schemes of Satan, we must learn to engage in spiritual warfare. Whether you know it or not, every day you engage in some form of warfare. The choice of loving someone who has hurt you, the choice of forgiving someone who has wronged you, the choice to try again after failing, the choice to let go of something you would like to hold on to, the choice to not believe the thoughts that are in your mind that contradict the word of God. If you have had make any of these decisions, then you have engaged in spiritual warfare.

You may say well I haven't fought any demons or been an intense battle. Well the basis of spiritual warfare is to over through the tactics and strategies the enemy uses in his attempt kill, steal and destroy. Some warfare may not be as simple as the examples used above, but the end result is the same…preventing the rooting of a seed that has stemmed from Satan. The first place warfare will begin is in your mind; Then your belief system, then your actions. If Satan can get control of your mind then he can tell you what to belief and then what you belief will become our actions. Satan knows the order of operation, mind over matter, belief over facts and action over acts. If he can control your operation then he can control your world. Even if you won't serve him, he'll settle for causing you to miss your destiny, causing you to miss your promised land, causing you to be ineffective in the kingdom, causing you to never reach your full potential.

So you ask how you engage in spiritual warfare- through seasons of love, hate, war, and peace. Matthew 11:12 says it like this, *"And from the days of John the Baptist until now the kingdom of God suffered violence and the violent take it by force"* (KJV). The violence that comes against the body of Christ is the continual attacks, schemes, and trickery Satan throws at those who are a part of the kingdom. Our warfare is not against any particular person in the flesh but against unseen forces operating through portals that are open through un-repented sin and acts which separate us from God, against a well-organized kingdom of counterfeits and manipulators. These forces are again not flesh and blood, but principalities, powers, rulers of darkness of this world, and spiritual wickedness in high places (Ephesians 6:12).

We cannot fight these forces with physical weapons but with the weapons of the word of God. With truth, with love, with binding and losing, with walking in authority and dominion, with captivating thoughts and bringing them under the submission of God. We fight with hating the things which are displeasing to the kingdom of God, with choosing to walk in peace, and purposely making every effort to destroy any work that goes against the principles of God. To violently take the kingdom authority of the kingdom of Satan we must purposefully, with a burning passion and efforts to be destructive and distorting every attack of Satan. We maintain our kingdom authority when we are able to strip Satan and his kingdom of workers from successfully completing their assignments in attacks against the kingdom.

Though there is some form or spiritual warfare in the believers life daily, there will be a time and season in your life where you will be entrusted with fighting a major spiritual battle. When you do you must remember that the kingdom of God is at stake. That their or souls or even on soul who may be at stake and saved through your warfare. There is a future and destiny that will be fulfilled because you chose to stay in the battle, because you chose to walk in kingdom authority, because you chose to fight even when you wanted to give up and everyone around you told you it was impossible to win the battle; Because you maintained control of your thoughts through the power of the Holy Spirit. Your warfare is your victory. All you have to do is stay in the battle to see it through to the end. God has graced and equipped your for battle. He would not send you in the field to fight if He knew you were not properly armed. You may not see the ammunition you possess, but God has a way of stirring up that which is places in you, especially when you cry out in times of desperation.

Have you found yourself repeating battles in your life? Have you seen yourself going through the same trial and situation repeatedly? Then I can assure you the battle is not over. You have given up on the battle or laid down your ammunition, but rest assured the battle remains even if you decide to leave the battle ground. God has a way of bringing you back. He gave you the battle because you are the one He has laid the ammunition in from the foundation of the world. He knows that if you don't fight this particular battle it won't get fought. Now don't be fooled, if you chose to continue to walk in disobedience and contrary to the will of God, He will assign someone else to the battle. Honestly, God doesn't need any of us to fight in these battles, but He chooses to work through the His children, He chooses to entrust His children to show His power and might. Ever scar, every bruise, every war wound you receive in the mist of your battle should be worn with pride; Pride of being, favored, chosen, and equipped to fight in such territory. When there is war raging in the land, armies only sends those soldiers who are trained and equipped for battle. The fact that you have even been chosen says just how you are seen in the sight of God. You are valuable to His work and he trusts your heart for him enough to enlist you for the assignment.

Feeling violent, then take it by force!
Purposefully chose to not only fight, but win.
Victory is within your purpose.
Put on the Whole Armor of God - Ephesians 6:13-17
If you want to engage in successful spiritual warfare, you must be equipped.
Here is your Armor:

Girt your lions with TRUTH

Put on your breastplate of RIGHTEOUSNESS

Shod your feet with the preparation of the GOSPEL OF PEACE

Take your shield of FAITH

Put on your helmet of SALVATION

Take your sword of the SPIRIT

Now that you have your armor, take a few minutes to search the word of God and write at least on scripture about each one. Memorize and meditate on it to help equip you for battle.

Part III

Harvest Time:
"Reaping What You have Sown in the Seasons"

Be not deceived; God is not mocked: for whatsoever a man soweth, that shall he also reap.

Galatians 6:7

Any farmer or anyone who has knowledge of the produce industry, understand that the earth's seasons are good for harvesting. They understand the nature of each season and can determine exactly what to do in each season to yield the harvest they desire. The premise of each season, the intended end, is to reach harvest time. The farmer knows when and what crop should be planted in which season. They know which soil each seed should be planted in. They know how to attend to the crop; How to prune, water, and watch over the crop. They don't plant the seeds of the crop and do all the tiling, all the pruning, watering, fertilizing, and watching in hopes that they may have crop in harvest season. No, they do all the work, go through all the processes EXPECTING the seeds to have reproduced crop in harvest season. They don't hope, they EXPECT crop! They EXPECT to see the fruit of their labor.

The same is true with each spiritual season we have just overviewed in Ecclesiastics 3. Just as there is a harvest for every season in the earth for reproduction, the same holds true for every spiritual season we experience. I know, I know you've heard this before. You've done the sowing, the tiling, and the plowing, endured the season even when you wanted to give up, and yet have not seen the harvest. Well my friend I have been there. When it seems as though you've done and are doing everything that you know is being required of you. You go through the season, but it seems there is no harvest. We'll let me ask, what is your EXPECTANCY?

I believe that the greatest reason we miss our harvest most often because our faith level in the midst of the seasons is not conducive to our expectancy. We say we believe, we go through the motions, but yet we waiver in our expectancy. Of course it's less heart breaking and emotional to not believe or not expect and receive nothing, than to expect everything and yet still receive nothing. The greatest lost in any season is having the worked in vein. Completing the season but not reaping the harvest because you failed to maintain your believe.

With the requirement of each season, there is a manifest harvest. Who would want to go through all the motions of requirements knowing that there is a promised reward, but never receive the reward; in the spiritual seasons of life; only those who have only hope with no expectancy will not receive the just reward and harvest of the passing of each season. Don't put in the work, and not expect to see your harvest. God is the god of promise and reward. Whatever he has spoken, He will perform. If he has told you to sow, to tile, to plow, you can be assured that He will reward you with the harvest of your labor.

What is Sowing?

Sowing is defined as scattering seed over the ground for growing (www.thefreedictionary.com). Sowing in done as the beginning process in the intent to make it to harvest or produce something. There are several ways of sowing and it is as equally important to know what type of seed you are sowing as it is the season in which you are sowing. When sowing seeds you must be aware of where the seed needs to be planted. What climate is necessary, what container is needed, if the seed can be planted directly into the ground, how to attend to the seed once planted. If the requirements are not followed you will not be able to receive the produce desired in harvest time.

So what does that say about our sowing spiritual seeds? The requirements are the same. We must know what seeds are to be sown in what season; Where to plant the seed most importantly and how to maintain the seed once it is planted. We find our instructions in the word of God. The word itself is the seed. Believe is the ground which it must be planted and faith is what will maintain the seed. God has given his children many promises. He has given some of us specific promises, prophecies, revelations; he has shown some of us our futures. So once you have that promise, you have your seed. The answer to rather you will receive your harvest or not is contingent on what you do with the seed.

The first step to take with your seed is to plant it. Put it in the ground. That is your security in knowing that that seed you have been giving will produce a harvest in due season.

Your believe system will determine is the ground you plant it in will produce your harvest or anything at all. Often God will speak to us give us a word or a promise. We get excited about the word. We trust the word, we believe the promise. Then the process begins. The ground gets a little hard, the soil get a little dry. Then we start to wonder about the seed. You know God said you are healed by his stripes, but yet you continue to get negative doctors reports. God tells you your family members will be saved but then you see then seemingly walking further and further way for anything that seems to be of God. God gives you a word pertaining to the increase of your finances, and then you lose your job. God promises you a home, but then you get the eviction notice.

Yes when you receive that promise the enemy will do all he can to make you believe that it will not come to pass. He will do all he can to make you doubt the seed that has been placed in your hand will ever produce a harvest. He wants you to believe that you have not received a seed of promise or word from God at all. See it is your belief that will cause you properly place your seed or misplace your seed. What you believe will determine what you will do. Your actions toward your seed will directly determine how you handle it. If you don't believe the promise or the word, then you cannot properly cultivate that seed in your life. Oh but only if you can chose to believe in your seed, you will be able to walk into total submission and obedience to God, and we know obedience brings the blessing.

Now once your seed is sown, once you chose to believe, then you can begin the process of cultivation, of nurturing your word to bring it to fruition and get ready for your harvest. Once you choose to believe the promise and word of God pertaining to your life, it will take faith to maintain and cultivate that word. Not just any little kind of faith, I'm talking about some unshakeable, crazy, don't make sense but I trust you kind of faith. It will take supernatural, spirit feed faith to see that seed to harvest time. Yep that muster seed faith- faith that can stand in the midst of any situation.

Don't think that the enemy will allow you to simple get your seed, plant it, cultivate it and sit back and watch you reap your harvest. No way. You better be prepared to till your ground daily. The enemy will do all he can to dry up your crop. He will send distractions, disillusions, contradictions your way every time you go to nurture your seed. He will even use those closest to your field to try and paint unbelief in your heart. If he can get you to a place of doubt, he knows you won't continue to nurture your seed. He knows you'll lose the drive to ensure your seed is maintained. He'll go as far as to attempt to make you believe that there will not be a harvest. But what do you do….you feed your seed with more seed, the word of God. Whenever you begin to feel doubt set in, you must recall the promise, recall the word. Remind yourself and remind your adversary that the word is true, that you believe it, and that you will do whatever it takes to maintain it. The power is in your hand and the harvest is yours. You must only maintain your seed.

Meditate on this passage of Scripture: Ecclesiastes 11:4-6 (NKJV)

4.) *He who observes the wind will not sow, and he who regards the clouds will not reap.*

5.) *As you do not know what is the way of*

the wind, or how the bones grow in the womb of her who is with child, So you do not know the works of God who makes everything.

6.) *In the morning sow your seed, And in the evening do not withhold your hand. For you do not know which will prosper, Either this or that, Or whether both alike will be good.*

~~~~~~~~~~~~~~~

We must not wait until we think conditions are favorable or the time is right for us to learn or figure out, or even begin to nurture our seeds. No matter what the situation or facts are regarding the promise and the word you must remember God's promises always supersede the facts. Act on faith and not on facts.

~~~~~~~~~~~~~~~

What seed has God given you?

✔ *Take a few minutes to write down the promises, prophecies, and words spoken over your life.*
✔ *Next to each one write what your belief is*

regarding that word.
✓ *Finally find a scripture of faith pertaining to your promise that will help you cultivate your seed when doubt tries to take over.*
If you complete this exercise you will have all you need to maintain your seed for harvest.

Reaping and Harvest

Now that you understand how God operates in His divine, triune power, understand the seasons and processes of life in the natural and spiritual aspects, understand your seed and how to plant and cultivate it to fruition, you can know go into your season of reaping and harvest. Before you can enjoy the reward of your labor let's first understand reaping and harvest. Be prepared to be blessed!

Reaping is defined as getting a return, recompense, or result; to gather or take up. **Harvest** is defined as the season when ripened crops are gathered; the crop or yield of one growing season; the result or consequence of any act, process, or event.

These definitions are so profound I decided to let them stand alone. But let's dig a little deeper into these definitions. Reaping guarantees a return recompense or reward; it insures that you will see results. It ensures that the bi-product of labor will come to your hands. This is the completion of the word of God over every promise, every prophesy, over every word spoken over your life. If you can maintain in the process, if you can grab a hold to everything God has spoken to you there is no doubt that you will see the results and receive your reward for making it through the seasons of pain, of turmoil, of joy and laughter, of losing and gaining, of mourning and joy.

Your seasons were only working for you a more exceedingly weight of glory that is in the form of your harvest. God will reward your faithfulness. You may say well I messed up. I even had to replant the seed more than once. That's okay we've all killed a few seeds in our life time. Be thankful that God gives that chance to plant that seed as many times as you need to get it to take root. But what you must remember is that God is not moved by your perfection, he is moved by your faith; If is your faith that yields the crop. Your expectancy that keeps you motivated to wait until harvest time.

Harvest, now this is where it really get good. The first definition of harvest is the season when ripened crops are gathered. Ok you can go ahead, take a minute and shout right there. Oh need me to tell you why. Well this says that the crops are ripened. Ever tried to eat an over ripe banana or any fruit that was not yet ripe. Well not so pleasant is it. Well in harvest time with God he will not release your crop until he knows it is ready for use, that it is suitable for your current state, that you are capable of handling the blessing. Matter of fact he will make sure that you're in the best place to reap the benefits of the harvest. Like at a table in the presence of your enemies, or in a hopeless situation, or at a time when you're ready to give up hope. He will ensure that your harvest is not only ready put that it will be of great benefit to you and those around you. He will make a believer out of those who couldn't see the blessing of your seasons. Who wanted you to give up or said you were maybe just a little bit crazy for believing what you did. One thing about harvest time, the fruit is always all so sweet.

The next definition of harvest says that it is the yield of one growing season. Okay feel free to shout again. This won't take long to break down, and not much needs to be said concerning this matter. Simply put, for every season you pass through, that you endure there is a harvest. So yes that means if you have passed through 2 seasons then there are at least portions of blessings for you. Each season bears its own fruit. No season is ended without the return of fruit during harvest time.

The last definition says harvest is the results or consequences of any act, process or event. As the old familiar saying goes, you reap just what you sow. Some call it karma, I call it harvest. Now just as cultivating and nurturing in seasons can lead you to production of harvest, the lack thereof will cause a lack of the full potential of receiving your harvest. If you do not properly maintain your seed, root in in the word of God and maintain it by faith, it is very well possible that it will not produce the harvest that was intended.

What you receive or yield in harvest is depicted by your course; if your course was maintained in hope or expectancy. If you're simply hoping over your seed you only believe that what you want can be had or that your harvest will come. If you have an expectancy about your seed, you not only believe that your will receive a harvest but you expect to see your harvest. Expectancy is what keeps your faith in tact when everything around you equates to you having a dead seed; when you are in expectancy, it just like waiting to give birth. You know that there is a due date but you also expect that that day will come. There is no doubt that you will give birth. There is no doubt that one day you will go into labor and the fruit of your womb will come forth. That's expectancy-knowing that there is an anticipated due date and patiently enduring the process to make it to the end. What are you expecting?

The Assurance of Harvest

Genesis 8:20-22 says, "And Noah built an alter unto the Lord; and took on every clean east, and of every clean fowl, and offered burnt offerings on the alter. And the Lord smelled a sweet savior; and the Lord said in his heart, I will not again curse the ground any more for man's sake; for the imagination of man's heart is evil from his youth; neither will I again smite any more everything living, as I have done. While the earth remained seedtime and harvest, and cold and heat, and summer and winter, and day and night shall not cease". (KJV)

Here is our blessed promise that we are assured that seedtime and harvest will remain in the earth; not only the harvesting but the seasons that are necessary to bring about the fruit. Once the sacrifice was made unto God, God made a covenant promise of things to remain in the earth. We know that this is a covenant due to the blood sacrifice that was made on the alter. And this covenant was again sealed with the sacrifice of the lamb Jesus Christ.

God is the same God yesterday today and forevermore. He is the God who was, who is, and who is to come. He is not a man that he should lie nor even have to repent. Whatever God promises you can rest assured that it is coming to pass. God has proven himself time and time again. Delivering the children of Israel to the Promised Land, Jesus rising form the dead, healing of the woman with the issue of blood. You can trust his word. You can trust his promise over your life. You can trust him to perform every word he has spoken over. It doesn't matter how radical or absurd God's promise may be in your life to others, root your promise in

believe, water it with faith, and get ready because when your season is over and your harvest is ripe, you will reap!
Insert your name:

This is
_____'s
Harvest

Are you at a point in your life where you feel as if your harvest will never come. That you may have missed or misheard what God has spoken to you. Don't marinate in your doubt but water your seed by remembering promises in your life that have already bought forth a harvest. Write down promises and harvest that have already taken place in your life.

Conclusion

It is inevitable that time will eventually expire on each and every one of our lives. Just as no man knows when the Son of God shall return, no one knows the exact time their life on earth will expire. It is essential for man to be cautious in the use and view of his time allotted daily.

Ephesians 5:15-17 reminds us that we live with power, understanding, and precision. It warns us, *"So be careful how you live. Don't live like fools, but like those who are wise. Make the most of every opportunity in these evil days. Don't act thoughtlessly, but understand what the Lord wants you to do"*.

The time that we are given, the days ahead may be filled with a mixture of pain and joy, of tears and happiness, of losing and gaining, mourning and rejoicing, but what we can grab hold to is the promise that everything is working in our favor. God desires to give you all he has intended for you. He desires to bless you abundantly; for you to be a mighty ad strong warrior for his kingdom. He desires that you fulfill your full potential. But in order to do so we must remember that we must fulfill the will of the father and not of the flesh. I God's will all things are perfect. They may not feel good or seem good but it is for the pruning of the saints, and the cultivating of souls.

God's word is undeniably true. It has been proved and tested throughout the ages of time. Truthfully even if there was no written account of the power of God and His power to fulfill promise, the fact that He spoke it is enough to active faith and gear up expectancy. Time is in the hands of God and him alone. He determines when it begins, when it ends and has the power to do as he will in between.

Let us heed the warnings and understand that our lives, every minute and second we are allotted daily do not belong to us to simply do as we will. But each minute is a gift that God has so graciously given us to be His hands and feet in the earth. God wants us to utilize our time in such a way that he may reveal himself to a lost and perverse world that is unconsciously yearning for a Savior and desires to be one with its creator. God doesn't need us to make his work complete- he has the power to make anything happen. But God loves us so much that he chooses to give us the opportunity to share in his power, love, and blessings. God is not blessed by the few minutes or years we dedicate to him, but we are blessed because God has chosen to give us an allotted period on earth to share in his divine works. The question is, what will you do with the time He has given you? I suggest you use it fulfilling the destiny He has set for you. Take it from me, it's far greater than any plan you can come up with and you will never be truly fulfilled until you're able to say, "I was born to do this".

Embrace who you are and choose to walk in destiny. The word of God is there to lead you along your journey in every season.
Simply embrace it; you're not alone of the journey!
S. O. S.

About the Author
Nathalie e. ford

Passionate, empowering, and encouraging are a few words to describe Author Nathalie E. Ford. Born and raised in Donaldsonville, LA, this small town girl has a passion to impact the world through her first passion, Ministering the uncompromised word of God, exposing the lies of the enemy, and empowering the kingdom of God through her gifts of writing and inspiration.

Nathalie is the daughter of Pastor Willie and Rachel Ford of Donaldsonville, LA and is a current resident of Lafayette, LA. Nathalie is a Minister of the gospel who strives not only to teach the word of God, but to live it day to day with the same excitement and joy that can be heard through her messages.

Nathalie purposes to impact the kingdom of God through the gift of writing, inspiration and wisdom by the leading of the Holy Spirit. Sharing insight, revelation and wisdom gained from her own journey through life and relationship with God, you can guarantee to be uplifted and empowered every time you engage in the work God's sends through her writings. Your life will be impacted and you will have a desire to know God more intimately. If you have not come to know God, be prepared to begin a new relationship that will change your life forever!

"If any man be in Christ, he is a new creature."
2 Corinthians 5:17

Booking:

Seasons of Singleness is not just another book for reading, but a ministry created to share revelation, wisdom and healing to those who have a cry for help.
To share teachings beyond the book, Seminars or Conferences are available to your organization or church. For additional information or for booking a "Seasons" Seminar or Conference, please contact:
Nathalie Ford at SeasonsofSingleness@gmail.com

www.ingramcontent.com/pod-product-compliance
Lightning Source LLC
Chambersburg PA
CBHW070307100426
42743CB00011B/2378